T0029815

The Penguin of ILHA GRANDE

For my mom, Diane—S. E.

To Rosa—R. A.

Text copyright © 2023 by Shannon Earle
Illustrations copyright © 2023 by Renato Alarcão
All rights reserved, including the right of reproduction in whole or in part in any form.
Charlesbridge and colophon are registered trademarks of Charlesbridge Publishing, Inc.

At the time of publication, all URLs printed in this book were accurate and active.
Charlesbridge, the author, and the illustrator are not responsible for the content or accessibility of any website.

Published by Charlesbridge
9 Galen Street, Watertown, MA 02472
(617) 926-0329
www.charlesbridge.com

Library of Congress Cataloging-in-Publication Data
Names: Earle, Shannon, author. | Alarcão, Renato, illustrator.
Title: The penguin of Ilha Grande: from animal rescue to extraordinary friendship / Shannon Earle;
   illustrated by Renato Alarcão.
Description: Watertown, MA: Charlesbridge, 2023. | Summary: "When an oil-covered penguin washes
   up in Brazil, Seu João saves its life. The man and penguin become friends, and the penguin won't return
   to the wild."—Provided by publisher.
Identifiers: LCCN 2019035071 (print) | LCCN 2019035072 (ebook) | ISBN 9781623541668 (hardcover) |
   ISBN 9781632899637 (ebook)
Subjects: LCSH: Dindim (Magellanic penguin)—Juvenile literature. | Souza, João Pereira de—Juvenile literature. |
   Magellanic penguin—Juvenile literature. | Magellanic penguin—Effect of oil spills on—Brazil—Juvenile literature. |
   Penguins—Juvenile literature. | Wildlife rescue—Brazil—Juvenile literature. | Human-animal relationships—Brazil—
   Juvenile literature.
Classification: LCC QL696.S473 E2245 2022 (print) | LCC QL696.S473 (ebook) | DDC 598.47—dc23
LC record available at https://lccn.loc.gov/2019035071
LC ebook record available at https://lccn.loc.gov/2019035072

Printed in China
(hc) 10 9 8 7 6 5 4 3 2 1

Illustrations done in watercolor, gouache, and colored pencils on Reciclatto paper
Display type handwritten and set in Badger by A. Pat Hickson
Text type set in Georgia by Matthew Carter
Printed by 1010 Printing International Limited in Huizhou, Guangdong, China
Production supervision by Jennifer Most Delaney
Designed by Kristen Nobles

The Penguin of ILHA GRANDE

FROM ANIMAL RESCUE TO EXTRAORDINARY FRIENDSHIP

Shannon Earle   *Illustrated by* Renato Alarcão

Charlesbridge

Every morning, Seu João drank his coffee, took a walk, and swam in the warm water of Praia Provetá in Brazil.

Then one day in May, he heard children shouting. Seu João rushed over to where they were gathered.

A penguin!

A little penguin lay on the beach, covered in black goo.

It could barely move.

Seu João carried the exhausted bird home. He tried to rinse away the thick oil. But the water ran off the slick, stuck-together feathers. The penguin's heart beat wildly.

Seu João tried dish soap. He patiently washed each feather. It worked!

Seu João's grandson asked about the "dindim." He was trying to say "pinguim," the Portuguese word for penguin.

Seu João smiled and named the penguin Dindim.

People in Provetá came to see Seu João's penguin. Local fishermen brought fresh sardines. The hungry penguin swallowed the fish whole. **Honk!**

Everyone loved Dindim, but if anyone other than Seu João tried to pet or feed him, the penguin pecked.

After two weeks Dindim was strong again—strong enough to go home.

Seu João loved Dindim, but he knew that penguins belong to the wild.

Seu João held Dindim on his lap one last time and stroked his sleek feathers. He fed Dindim one last sardine and walked with him to the water's edge. He gave the penguin a tiny push.

Dindim dove into the water and splashed in the waves. But then he swam right back to Seu João. **_Honk!_**

Seu João's heart thumped with joy and sorrow.

The next day, Seu João took Dindim far out to sea in a fishing boat.

He placed his hand on Dindim's head and looked into his shiny black eyes.

He placed Dindim in the water and took the boat back to shore. Seu João didn't know if he would ever see Dindim again. He returned home . . .

. . . and there was Dindim! *Honk!*

After that, Dindim stayed with Seu João. Every day Seu João brought fresh fish. Every day they swam together in the ocean. And every day they showered together in the little blue house.

For many months Dindim slept in the yard. The gate was open, and the path to the ocean was clear. Still Dindim stayed.

One hot day in February, Dindim's feathers began to fall out. Every
day Dindim lost more of his ragged, worn-out feathers. He became a very
lumpy-looking penguin.

Seu João worried that Dindim was sick. Dindim wouldn't eat, swim,
or take showers. Seu João didn't know what to do.

A few weeks later Dindim started growing new feathers. It took almost three weeks, but finally, right in time for Carnaval, Dindim had a shiny new coat. He was waterproof again and ready to swim.

Dindim was different. He stopped sitting on Seu João's lap. Every morning he swallowed his sardines and went straight to the beach to swim.

One day Dindim dove into the water with Seu João as usual. But this time Dindim swam deeper and farther than before.

Seu João tried to keep up, but his arms grew tired. He had to turn back.

He stood at the edge of the beach. He waited for a long time. Only waves splashed against the shore.

Dindim was gone.

Seu João trudged back across the sand to his little blue house.
Silence echoed against the concrete walls as he took a shower and ate
his dinner. He lay in bed, listening for the *flap-flap* of Dindim's wet
webbed feet and a hello honk. But all he heard were geckos in the night.

The next morning Seu João sat and drank his coffee. His lap was empty. But he remembered Dindim's silky feathers and the beat of his heart.

Seu João walked on the beach and swam in the ocean, looking and listening for Dindim. Birds circled and cawed in the sky, but no penguins honked on Provetá Beach.

The village children asked where Dindim was.

Seu João just shook his head.

One morning four months later, as Seu João stood digging his toes in the sand, he heard a sound that made his heart pound like the waves on the shore.

Honk! Honk!

Seu João peered down the beach.

Could it really be?

Dindim! The penguin waddled as fast as his little legs could carry him, right into Seu João's arms. The two touched bill to nose.

When they got back home, Seu João gave Dindim twelve fat sardines, one after the other. Then Dindim headed straight to the shower. *Honk!*

Dindim lived with Seu João for seven years. They swam together, showered together, ate together, and walked on the beach together.

Each year, Dindim changed his feathers, honked goodbye, and headed to sea. For four months he lived in the wild. No one knows exactly where he went. But every year, right before Seu João's birthday in June, Dindim came home.

"Nunca vi como é que um bicho que vive no mar
se pega com uma pessoa como esse bicho se pegô comigo."

* * *

"I'd never imagined how a creature that lives in the sea
could get as attached to a person as this animal got attached to me."

—SEU JOÃO PEREIRA DE SOUZA

Where Is Dindim Now?

In 2018, after seven years, Dindim did not return to Provetá. There are many possible explanations. Dindim was a young penguin when Seu João first found him. After many years with his human friend, Dindim may have gotten old enough to look for a mate. He might now spend his summers raising chicks of his own. He may spend his winters farther south, closer to where he breeds. It is also possible that something happened to Dindim. Penguins in the wild face many dangers, from predators to oil spills. Most wild penguins who survive to breeding age like Dindim live ten years or more, so we hope that Dindim is alive and well, wherever he is.

Magellanic Penguins

Dindim is a Magellanic penguin, named for the explorer Ferdinand Magellan, who first described the species. From September to March—spring and summer in the southern hemisphere—Magellanic penguins breed in large colonies on the coasts of Argentina, the Falkland Islands (Islas Malvinas), and Chile, in an area known as Patagonia. Penguin families live in burrows or under shrubs, and both parents help incubate the eggs and raise one or two chicks.

Once they grow feathers, chicks leave the colony in January and February. After the chicks head north, the adults fatten up before coming ashore to molt—changing their old feathers for new ones. Penguins don't eat during their annual molt. By April or May most adults head to the ocean to hunt for fish, squid, and crustaceans. Winter foraging can take hungry Magellanic penguins as far north as Brazil in search of prey.

Penguins in the *Spheniscus* genus—including Magellanic penguins and their relatives the Humboldt, African, and Galapagos penguins—have white stripes and often black feathers on their chests that look like spots. Scientists aren't sure whether the white stripe that circles the penguins' eyes and the black stripe around their white belly help these penguins hunt together, but some think they might. Fish swimming in schools, such as anchovies and sardines, sometimes break formation when they see stripes. No one knows exactly why. But we do know that when fish leave a school, they are much easier to catch.

Penguins swallow their food whole and alive while they are swimming underwater. Their tongue and the back of their throat are covered in tiny barbed projections that point toward their stomach, which helps keep squirming squid and fish from escaping. Some penguins eat small rocks either to crush the fish bones in their stomach or to make them feel full. In the spring they eat shells, which give them calcium to make strong eggshells that protect their offspring.

Threats and Conservation

The IUCN (International Union for Conservation of Nature) lists Magellanic penguins as a Near Threatened species. One of the main threats to penguins is oil. Large ships sometimes leak or release oil into the ocean. Offshore drilling can also cause oil spills. Penguins do not see the oil until they swim into it. Oil separates feathers so the penguins are no longer waterproof. Without their waterproof feathers, penguins can get too cold. They can no longer swim well or catch fish. In the 1980s more than forty thousand Magellanic penguins died each year from oil in the ocean. People lobbied to change the laws about where big ships could travel so penguins could have safer routes in the ocean. Petroleum pollution is still a problem, but changing the shipping lanes has made the ocean safer for penguins. Magellanic penguin deaths from oil spills in southern Argentina are now rare.

Anchovies are one of Magellanic penguins' favorite foods. Humans also fish for anchovies, and when we take too many, penguins have to work harder and some die of starvation. Penguins can also get caught and tangled in fishing nets and drown. The Punta Tombo Marine Protected Area in Argentina protects the ocean near a major nesting site where many penguins swim and feed in summer. Setting limits on how many fish people can catch helps both penguins and fishermen. Protected areas, on land and at sea, keep nesting and feeding sites safer. There are not yet any protected areas on Magellanic penguins' wintering grounds.

Plastic in the ocean is another big threat to seabirds like penguins, which sometimes mistake plastic for food. When birds eat plastic, their stomachs fill up with trash and they are unable to eat real food. Penguins can also get plastic caught around their feet or necks.

Climate change is also a threat to penguins. Extreme weather events are becoming more frequent and severe. Strong storms cause heavy rains that flood or collapse penguin burrows. Chicks die if they get too wet, too cold, or too hot. Adults can die in extreme heat. Scientists are still learning about all the ways the climate crisis is harming penguins. There are many ways people can take action against climate change. Reducing energy use and switching to solar, wind, and hydro power instead of fossil fuels are major changes families and countries can make.

What You Can Do

The most important thing you can do is support conservation and science. Learn more about penguins and other threatened and endangered species and become a member of a conservation organization that protects penguins and their habitats. Kids can be conservation leaders in their families, schools, and communities. You can research on the internet how to reduce your carbon footprint, eliminate single-use plastics, and eat sustainably caught seafood to help penguins and the planet. When kids speak up about protecting the Earth, adults also listen, learn, and change.

Glossary

Dindim (jeen-jeem): A *d* before an *i* or an *e* in Portuguese makes a sound similar to the *j* sound in English. Seu João's grandson couldn't pronounce the Portuguese word for penguin. He asked "Cadê o dindim?" (Where is the penguin?) That's how Dindim got his name.

pinguim (ping-weem): penguin.

Praia Provetá, Ilha Grande (PRY-ya pro-vet-AH, EEL-ya GRAN-jee): Provetá Beach is on the west end of Ilha Grande (Big Island) off the coast of Brazil in the state of Rio de Janeiro. It is Seu João's home.

Seu João (SAY-u Ju-OW): *Seu* is a short form of *senhor*, which means "mister" in Brazilian Portuguese. *Seu* before *João* is a polite but familiar address, like saying Mr. John in English. Senhor Pereira de Souza is more formal.

Writing This Story

I first heard of Dindim and Seu João when their story became international news. A biologist-photographer named João Krajewski was the first to share their story with the world. I read many news stories about Dindim on outlets like CNN, NBC, BBC, and the *Independent*. Since I speak Portuguese, I also watched an interview with both Seu João (whose full name is João Pereira de Souza) and João Krajewski on Brazilian TV. I wrote to João Krajewski, who shared more details, reviewed an early draft of this story, and helped me reach out to Seu João's daughter.

I also read a lot about Magellanic penguins. The Global Penguin Society, BirdLife International, Smithsonian magazine, National Geographic, and Conservation Biology were some of my sources. Dr. Dee Boersma heads the Center for Ecosystem Sentinels at the University of Washington and has worked with Magellanic penguins at Punta Tombo for more than thirty-five years. She reviewed the story, especially the penguin facts. Her website, www.ecosystemsentinels.org, has information and short videos about Magellanic penguin biology, research, and conservation. To find out more, search for "Dindim penguin" online.